BENEATH
THE RUBBLE
STUDY GUIDE

HOW TO GET THE MOST OUT OF THIS STUDY GUIDE

Welcome to the study guide for "Beneath the Rubble"! This guide is designed to help you delve deeper into the powerful lessons and reflections from Sheldon and Annette's journey. Here are some tips to help you maximize your experience and gain the most from each chapter:

1 PARTNER UP
Consider going through this study guide with a friend, family member, or small group. Sharing insights, discussing questions, and praying together can enhance your experience and provide mutual encouragement and support.

2 SET ASIDE DEDICATED TIME
Allocate specific times each day or week to work through the lessons. Consistency will help you stay committed and allow for deep reflection on each chapter's content.

3 BE HONEST AND OPEN
As you answer reflection questions and journal, be sincere with yourself and God. Authenticity in your responses will lead to greater personal growth and spiritual breakthroughs.

4 PRAY FOR GUIDANCE
Start each session with prayer, asking God to open your heart and mind to His truths. Invite the Holy Spirit to guide your thoughts and reflections as you work through the lessons.

5 REFLECT AND APPLY
Take time not only to reflect on the questions but also to think about how you can apply the lessons to your daily life. Real transformation happens when we put what we learn into practice.

6 KEEP A JOURNAL
Use a separate journal or notebook to write down your thoughts, prayers, and insights. This will allow you to look back and see how God has been working in your life throughout this study.

7 **ENGAGE WITH SCRIPTURE**
Each chapter includes a key Bible verse. Spend time reading and meditating on these scriptures, allowing God's Word to speak directly to your heart.

8 **SHARE YOUR JOURNEY**
Feel free to share what you're learning with others, whether through conversation, social media, or a personal blog. Sharing your journey can inspire and encourage others in their faith.

9 **BE PATIENT WITH YOURSELF**
Spiritual growth is a process. Be patient with yourself as you navigate through the lessons, and trust that God is working in you, even if the progress seems slow.

10 **SEEK FURTHER UNDERSTANDING**
If a particular topic or scripture resonates with you, take the time to study it further. Use additional resources like commentaries, podcasts, or books to deepen your understanding.

By following these tips, you'll be well on your way to making the most of this study guide for "Beneath the Rubble." Remember, this journey is about growing closer to God, understanding His love and grace, and experiencing His transformative power in your life. Enjoy the journey and embrace the changes God brings along the way!

THE AWAKENING

Have you ever experienced a moment that made you question everything you thought you knew about your life and family? In this lesson, we'll explore how such pivotal moments can lead to deep reflections on our past and the search for approval and love. As we journey through Sheldon's story, we'll see how God's love and affirmation can transform our lives and provide hope for the future.

Psalm 27:10 (NLT):
"Even if my father and mother abandon me, the Lord will hold me close."

In this chapter, we see Sheldon's life turned upside down when the FBI arrives at his home, leading him to reflect on his past. His childhood was marked by a constant search for approval and love from his parents, who struggled to show affection due to their own unresolved issues. This lack of affirmation deeply affected his relationships and choices throughout life. The chapter highlights the importance of parental guidance and the lasting impact of our early experiences.

If you haven't read Chapter One, go do so now.

QUESTIONS FOR REFLECTION:

1. How did Sheldon's childhood experiences shape his view of love and approval?

2. What were some of the significant events in Sheldon's early years that influenced his relationships?

3. How did Sheldon's parents' inability to show affection affect his behavior and decisions?

4. How did Sheldon's relationship with Annette provide him with the affirmation he longed for?

5. What were some of the consequences of Sheldon's neediness in his relationship with Annette?

PERSONAL REFLECTION QUESTIONS:

1. Reflect on your childhood. How did your parents show love and approval? How has this impacted your adult relationships?

2. In what ways have you sought approval from others? How has this affected your self-worth and decisions?

3. Consider a time when you felt the most loved and affirmed. What was significant about that experience, and how did it shape your understanding of love?

4. How can you seek God's approval and affirmation in your life instead of relying solely on the approval of others?

5. What steps can you take to ensure that you show love and affirmation to those around you, especially your family members?

ASK GOD TO SPEAK TO YOU:

Take a moment to pray and reflect on the areas of your life where you seek approval from others. Ask God to reveal any wounds from your past that need healing and to help you find your worth and affirmation in Him. Write down any thoughts or impressions you receive during this time of reflection.

NEXT STEPS:

1 PRAYER: Pray for God's healing in areas where you feel abandoned or unloved. Ask Him to help you find your worth and affirmation in His love.

2 SHARE: Talk with a trusted friend or mentor about your reflections and insights from this chapter. Discuss how you can support each other in seeking God's approval and showing love to those around you.

3 ACT: Identify one practical way you can show love and affirmation to someone in your life this week. It could be a family member, friend, or colleague. Make a deliberate effort to express appreciation and support.

4 REFLECT: What did God tell you to do? Write down your next steps and commit to following through.

5 JOURNAL: Spend 10-15 minutes journaling about your childhood experiences and how they have shaped your adult life. Reflect on the key verse and how it applies to your situation.

THE VOID

Have you ever felt that despite having everything you thought you wanted, there was still something missing? In this lesson, we'll delve into Sheldon's realization that material success and relationships cannot fill the void in our hearts. We'll explore how God's love and purpose provide the true fulfillment we seek and offer hope for overcoming our deepest struggles.

John 4:13-14 (NLT):
"Jesus replied, 'Anyone who drinks this water will soon become thirsty again. But those who drink the water I give will never be thirsty again. It becomes a fresh, bubbling spring within them, giving them eternal life.'"

In this chapter, Sheldon finds himself struggling with the realities of marriage and the void in his heart that nothing seems to fill. Despite having the woman of his dreams, he realizes that his heart still yearns for something more. Both Sheldon and Annette deal with their past traumas and lack of understanding about relationships and God's purpose for sex, leading to many trials and misunderstandings. This chapter highlights the deep-seated need for God's love and guidance in our lives, especially in our relationships.

If you haven't read Chapter Two, go do so now.

QUESTIONS FOR REFLECTION:

1. How did Sheldon's expectations of marriage differ from the reality he experienced?

2. What were some of the challenges Sheldon and Annette faced in their relationship due to their past experiences?

3. How did Sheldon's upbringing influence his views on marriage and relationships?

4. In what ways did Sheldon's need for approval and affirmation affect his behavior and decisions in his marriage?

5. How did the constant moving and financial instability impact Sheldon and Annette's family life?

PERSONAL REFLECTION QUESTIONS:

1. Reflect on your own relationships. How have your past experiences shaped your expectations and interactions with others?

2. In what ways have you sought fulfillment in things or people rather than in God? How has that impacted your sense of satisfaction and peace?

3. Consider a time when you faced significant challenges in a relationship. How did you handle it, and what did you learn from that experience?

4. How can you invite God into your relationships to provide guidance, healing, and fulfillment?

5. What steps can you take to better understand and communicate your needs and expectations in your relationships?

ASK GOD TO SPEAK TO YOU:

Take a moment to pray and reflect on the areas of your life where you seek fulfillment outside of God. Ask God to reveal any voids in your heart that need His love and to guide you in finding true satisfaction in Him. Write down any thoughts or impressions you receive during this time of reflection.

NEXT STEPS:

1 **PRAYER:** Pray for God's guidance in areas where you feel a void or lack of fulfillment. Ask Him to fill those voids with His love and purpose.

2 **SHARE:** Talk with a trusted friend or mentor about your reflections and insights from this chapter. Discuss how you can support each other in seeking God's fulfillment in your lives.

3 **ACT:** Identify one practical way you can improve your relationships this week. It could be through better communication, showing appreciation, or seeking reconciliation where needed.

4 **REFLECT:** What did God tell you to do? Write down your next steps and commit to following through.

5 **JOURNAL:** Spend 10-15 minutes journaling about your experiences and how they have shaped your understanding of relationships. Reflect on the key verse and how it applies to your situation.

HANGING IN THE BALANCE

Have you ever faced a period in your life where everything seemed to be falling apart? In this lesson, we'll explore how Sheldon navigated the intense challenges leading up to his trial and the relentless attacks on his family and business. Despite the chaos, glimmers of hope and God's intervention shine through, reminding us that He is always present, even in our darkest times.

Isaiah 41:10 (NLT):
"*Don't be afraid, for I am with you. Don't be discouraged, for I am your God. I will strengthen you and help you. I will hold you up with my victorious right hand.*"

In this chapter, Sheldon escapes prison but finds himself still imprisoned by the chaos and challenges in his life. The next eighteen months leading up to his trial are filled with relentless attacks from a former employee, Draven, who seeks to destroy Sheldon's business and family. Despite these attacks, moments of divine intervention and hope appear, showing God's presence and support even when Sheldon isn't actively seeking Him.

If you haven't read Chapter Three, go do so now.

QUESTIONS FOR REFLECTION:

1. How did Aaron discover Draven's plans to destroy Sheldon's business?

2. What were some of the threats and attacks Draven made against Sheldon and his family?

3. How did Sheldon and his family respond to the workers' comp issue, and what unexpected help did they receive?

4. How did the extortion and constant attacks impact Sheldon's mental and emotional state?

5. What role did Sheldon's lawyer, Harry, play in protecting Sheldon from threats?

PERSONAL REFLECTION QUESTIONS:

1. Reflect on a time when you faced relentless challenges. How did you handle the pressure, and what helped you persevere?

2. In what ways have you seen God intervene in your life during difficult times, even when you weren't actively seeking Him?

3. Consider a situation where you felt hopeless. How did you find the strength to keep going, and what role did your faith play in that process?

4. How can you rely more on God's strength and promises during times of uncertainty and attack?

5. What steps can you take to strengthen your relationship with God and recognize His presence in your daily struggles?

ASK GOD TO SPEAK TO YOU:

Take a moment to pray and reflect on the areas of your life where you feel under attack or overwhelmed. Ask God to reveal His presence and guidance in these situations and to strengthen your faith in His promises. Write down any thoughts or impressions you receive during this time of reflection.

NEXT STEPS:

1 **PRAYER:** Pray for God's protection and guidance in areas where you feel attacked or overwhelmed. Ask Him to strengthen your faith and provide clarity and peace.

2 **SHARE:** Talk with a trusted friend or mentor about your reflections and insights from this chapter. Discuss how you can support each other in seeking God's guidance and protection in your lives.

3 **ACT:** Identify one practical way you can rely on God's promises this week. It could be through reading scripture, praying, or seeking fellowship with other believers.

....

....

....

....

4 **REFLECT:** What did God tell you to do? Write down your next steps and commit to following through.

....

....

....

....

5 **JOURNAL:** Spend 10-15 minutes journaling about your experiences and how they have shaped your understanding of God's presence in your life. Reflect on the key verse and how it applies to your situation.

JUDGEMENT DAY

Have you ever faced a moment when your entire future seemed to hang in the balance? In this lesson, we'll explore Sheldon's sentencing hearing and the overwhelming anxiety and fear that accompanied it. Despite the dire circumstances, Sheldon experiences a miraculous turn of events that reveals God's grace and intervention in his life, offering hope for even the most hopeless situations.

Romans 8:28 (NLT): *"And we know that God causes everything to work together for the good of those who love God and are called according to his purpose for them."*

In this chapter, Sheldon faces his sentencing hearing with the expectation of going to prison. The weight of his past actions and the reality of the consequences finally break him. However, in a surprising turn of events, the judge grants him probation instead of prison time, marking a pivotal moment of grace and a new beginning. Sheldon realizes the depth of God's love and begins to see his life from a different perspective.

If you haven't read Chapter Four, go do so now.

QUESTIONS FOR REFLECTION:

1. What news did Sheldon's defense attorney share with him before the sentencing hearing, and how did it impact Sheldon?

2. How did Sheldon's church view public prayer, and how did this influence the pastor's prayer for Sheldon?

3. Describe Sheldon's emotional state during the sentencing hearing. How did he feel about his past actions and their consequences?

4. What was the judge's final decision, and how did it differ from what Sheldon expected?

5. How did Sheldon's perception of God change after the judge's verdict?

PERSONAL REFLECTION QUESTIONS:

1. Reflect on a time when you faced a situation where the outcome seemed certain and unfavorable. How did you cope with the anxiety and fear?

2. In what ways have you experienced God's grace in your life during difficult times? How did it change your perspective?

3. Consider a moment when you felt completely broken or defeated. How did you find hope and strength to move forward?

4. How can you trust in God's plan and purpose for your life, even when circumstances seem bleak?

5. What steps can you take to deepen your relationship with God and recognize His presence in your daily struggles?

ASK GOD TO SPEAK TO YOU:

Take a moment to pray and reflect on the areas of your life where you feel overwhelmed or hopeless. Ask God to reveal His grace and purpose in these situations and to strengthen your faith in His promises. Write down any thoughts or impressions you receive during this time of reflection.

NEXT STEPS:

1 PRAYER: Pray for God's guidance and strength in areas where you feel overwhelmed or defeated. Ask Him to show you His purpose and to fill you with His peace.

2 SHARE: Talk with a trusted friend or mentor about your reflections and insights from this chapter. Discuss how you can support each other in seeking God's grace and purpose in your lives.

3 ACT: Identify one practical way you can trust in God's plan this week. It could be through prayer, reading scripture, or seeking fellowship with other believers.

4 REFLECT: What did God tell you to do? Write down your next steps and commit to following through.

5 JOURNAL: Spend 10-15 minutes journaling about your experiences and how they have shaped your understanding of God's grace and intervention. Reflect on the key verse and how it applies to your situation.

ROAD TO RECOVERY

Have you ever faced a journey of healing and restoration that seemed impossible? In this lesson, we'll explore Sheldon's difficult path to mending relationships with his children and overcoming deep-rooted issues within his family. As he begins to understand the importance of pursuing his children's hearts and dealing with his past, we see how God's grace continues to guide him towards true recovery.

Psalm 147:3 (NLT):
"He heals the broken-hearted and bandages their wounds."

In this chapter, Sheldon realizes the depth of pain he has caused his children and begins the arduous journey of healing and recovery. Through counseling and the support of his family, Sheldon starts to understand the importance of pursuing his children's hearts and addressing the root causes of his behavior. Despite setbacks and challenges, the process brings about significant growth and transformation.

If you haven't read Chapter Five, go do so now.

QUESTIONS FOR REFLECTION:

1. What prompted Melinda and Aaron to confront Sheldon about the pain he had caused them?

2. How did Sheldon initially react to the idea of going to counseling, and what changed his mind?

3. What realization did Sheldon have about his own needs and how they affected his relationships with his children?

4. How did the conference with Melinda help Sheldon understand his own brokenness and the root of his actions?

5. What steps did Sheldon take towards healing and building a better relationship with his family?

PERSONAL REFLECTION QUESTIONS:

1. Reflect on a time when you had to confront painful issues in your relationships. How did you respond, and what did you learn from the experience?

....

....

2. In what ways have you sought healing and recovery from past hurts? How has God been a part of that journey?

....

....

3. Consider the relationships in your life that need healing. What steps can you take to pursue the hearts of those you love?

....

....

4. How can you rely on God's grace and strength as you work towards healing and recovery in your life?

....

....

5. What practical steps can you take to address deep-rooted issues and build stronger, healthier relationships?

....

....

Beneath The Rubble Study Guide

ASK GOD TO SPEAK TO YOU:

Take a moment to pray and reflect on the areas of your life where you need healing and recovery. Ask God to reveal any wounds that need His touch and to guide you in the steps you need to take towards restoration. Write down any thoughts or impressions you receive during this time of reflection.

NEXT STEPS:

1 PRAYER: Pray for God's guidance and strength in areas where you need healing. Ask Him to help you pursue the hearts of those you love and to provide the grace needed for restoration.

2 SHARE: Talk with a trusted friend or mentor about your reflections and insights from this chapter. Discuss how you can support each other in seeking God's healing and recovery in your lives.

3 ACT: Identify one practical way you can work towards healing a relationship this week. It could be through honest communication, seeking counseling, or taking steps to understand and address past hurts.

4 REFLECT: What did God tell you to do? Write down your next steps and commit to following through.

5 JOURNAL: Spend 10-15 minutes journaling about your experiences and how they have shaped your understanding of healing and recovery. Reflect on the key verse and how it applies to your situation.

SOAR: AS WRITTEN BY ANNETTE

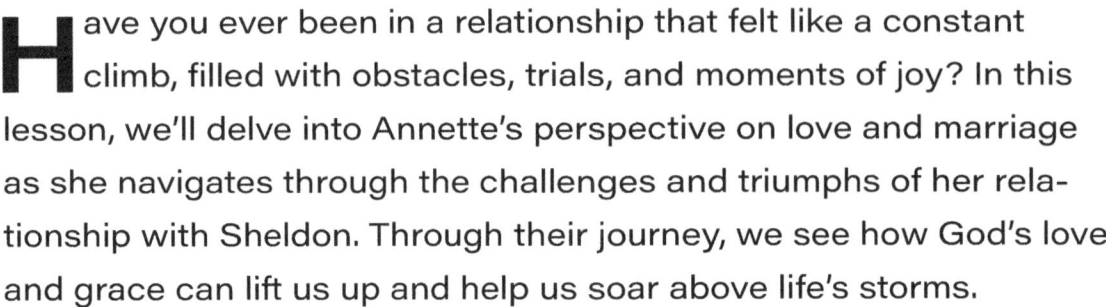

Have you ever been in a relationship that felt like a constant climb, filled with obstacles, trials, and moments of joy? In this lesson, we'll delve into Annette's perspective on love and marriage as she navigates through the challenges and triumphs of her relationship with Sheldon. Through their journey, we see how God's love and grace can lift us up and help us soar above life's storms.

Isaiah 40:31 (NLT):
"But those who trust in the Lord will find new strength. They will soar high on wings like eagles. They will run and not grow weary. They will walk and not faint."

In this chapter, Annette shares her experience of dealing with feelings of unworthiness, rejection, and the challenges of marriage. She recounts a profound encounter with God that transformed her heart and marriage, bringing healing and a renewed sense of love and commitment.

If you haven't read Chapter Six, go do so now.

QUESTIONS FOR REFLECTION:

1. What prompted Annette to question Sheldon about his involvement with pornography, and how did his response affect her?

2. How did the devotional reading on Isaiah 40 impact Annette and Sheldon's marriage?

3. What were some of the challenges Annette faced in her relationship with Sheldon, and how did she overcome them?

4. How did Annette's encounter with God during the devotional reading bring healing to her heart and marriage?

5. What steps did Annette take to maintain and nurture her relationship with Sheldon after their vow renewal?

PERSONAL REFLECTION QUESTIONS:

1. Reflect on a time when you faced significant challenges in a relationship. How did you navigate through those challenges, and what did you learn from the experience?

2. In what ways have you experienced God's grace and love lifting you up during difficult times?

3. Consider the importance of trust and communication in your relationships. How can you work towards building and maintaining these aspects?

4. How does the key verse, Isaiah 40:31, apply to your current life situation? What areas do you need to trust in the Lord for renewed strength?

5. What practical steps can you take to soar above the storms in your life and see from a heavenly perspective?

ASK GOD TO SPEAK TO YOU:

Take a moment to pray and reflect on the areas of your life where you need God's strength and perspective. Ask God to reveal any lies or obstacles that are preventing you from soaring above your circumstances. Write down any thoughts or impressions you receive during this time of reflection.

NEXT STEPS:

1   **PRAYER:** Pray for God's guidance and strength in areas where you need to overcome challenges. Ask Him to help you see from a heavenly perspective and to soar above the storms in your life.

2   **SHARE:** Talk with a trusted friend or mentor about your reflections and insights from this chapter. Discuss how you can support each other in seeking God's strength and perspective in your relationships.

3   **ACT:** Identify one practical way you can work towards building trust and communication in a key relationship this week. It could be through honest conversations, seeking counseling, or taking steps to address and heal past hurts.

4   **REFLECT:** What did God tell you to do? Write down your next steps and commit to following through.

5   **JOURNAL:** Spend 10-15 minutes journaling about your experiences and how they have shaped your understanding of trust and perseverance. Reflect on the key verse and how it applies to your situation.

HEALING WATERS

Have you ever felt unworthy of love or struggled with finding your identity outside of your achievements? In this lesson, we'll explore the journey of understanding our true worth and identity in Christ. Through Sheldon's story, we see how God's love and grace can transform our perception of ourselves and our purpose.

Psalms 127:1-2 (NLT): *"Unless the Lord builds a house, the work of the builders is wasted. Unless the Lord protects a city, guarding it with sentries will do no good. It is useless for you to work so hard from early morning until late at night, anxiously working for food to eat; for God gives rest to his loved ones."*

In this chapter, Sheldon and Annette reflect on their personal struggles, how they affected their family and business, and how surrendering to God brought healing and restoration. Their story emphasizes the importance of relying on God's strength and guidance rather than our own efforts.

If you haven't read Chapter Seven, go do so now.

QUESTIONS FOR REFLECTION:

1. How did Sheldon's identity and emotions tied to his business affect his relationship with his family?

2. What were the three things Janna asked Sheldon to do to help rebuild their business?

3. How did Sheldon learn to surrender control and trust God with his business?

4. What challenges did Annette face in her marriage with Sheldon, and how did she cope with them?

5. How did the concept of "labor into rest" play a role in Sheldon's transformation?

PERSONAL REFLECTION QUESTIONS:

1. Reflect on a time when you struggled to let go of control. How did that impact your relationships and well-being?

2. How can you practice surrendering control to God in your daily life?

3. Consider the role of expectations in your relationships. How can you adjust your expectations to foster healthier interactions?

4. What steps can you take to create a balance between your personal, professional, and spiritual life?

5. How does the key verse, Psalms 127:1-2, resonate with your current life situation?

ASK GOD TO SPEAK TO YOU:

Take a moment to pray and reflect on the areas of your life where you need to surrender control and trust God. Ask Him to reveal any strongholds or obstacles that are preventing you from experiencing His peace and rest. Write down any thoughts or impressions you receive during this time of reflection.

NEXT STEPS:

1 **PRAYER:** Pray for God's guidance and strength in areas where you need to let go of control. Ask Him to help you rest in His love and provision.

2 **SHARE:** Talk with a trusted friend or mentor about your reflections and insights from this chapter. Discuss how you can support each other in seeking God's strength and perspective in your relationships.

3 **ACT:** Identify one practical way you can practice surrendering control this week. It could be through delegating tasks, spending time in prayer, or taking a break from work to rest.

....

....

....

....

4 **REFLECT:** What did God tell you to do? Write down your next steps and commit to following through.

....

....

....

....

5 **JOURNAL:** Spend 10-15 minutes journaling about your experiences and how they have shaped your understanding of surrender and trust. Reflect on the key verse and how it applies to your situation.

EDGE OF DESPAIR

Have you ever faced a situation so dire that you felt you were standing on the edge of despair? In this lesson, Sheldon and Annette share their experiences of confronting severe health challenges and how they navigated these trials with faith and resilience.

Psalms 23:4 (NLT): *"Even when I walk through the darkest valley, I will not be afraid, for you are close beside me. Your rod and your staff protect and comfort me."*

In this chapter, Sheldon and Annette recount how they felt God's presence and protection throughout their ordeals. Their story emphasizes the significance of trusting in God's presence during our darkest moments and the transformative power of prayer and communion in bringing healing and hope..

If you haven't read Chapter Eight, go do so now.

QUESTIONS FOR REFLECTION:

1. What were the conflicting medical advices Sheldon received initially, and how did it affect his decision-making process?

2. How did Sheldon's high pain tolerance impact his response to his health crisis?

3. How did taking communion and praying as a family play a role in Sheldon's recovery?

4. What was the significance of Sheldon's experience with Dr. Crandall?

5. How did Sheldon's past emotional trauma potentially contribute to his physical health issues?

PERSONAL REFLECTION QUESTIONS:

1. Reflect on a time when you faced a health crisis. How did you navigate the situation, and what role did your faith play in it?

2. How can you incorporate the practice of communion and prayer into your daily life for spiritual and physical healing?

3. Consider the support system around you. How can you strengthen your community of faith to provide support during challenging times?

4. What steps can you take to address unresolved emotional pain that might be affecting your physical health?

5. How does the key verse, Psalms 23:4, resonate with your current life situation?

ASK GOD TO SPEAK TO YOU:

Take a moment to pray and reflect on any health challenges or emotional pain you might be experiencing. Ask God to reveal any areas where you need His healing touch and guidance. Write down any thoughts or impressions you receive during this time of reflection.

NEXT STEPS:

1 **PRAYER:** Pray for God's healing and guidance in areas where you need physical and emotional restoration. Ask Him to help you trust His presence and protection.

2 **SHARE:** Talk with a trusted friend or mentor about your reflections and insights from this chapter. Discuss how you can support each other in seeking God's healing and strength during health crises.

3 **ACT:** Identify one practical way you can incorporate the practice of communion and prayer into your daily routine for spiritual and physical well-being.

4 **REFLECT:** What did God tell you to do? Write down your next steps and commit to following through.

5 **JOURNAL:** Spend 10-15 minutes journaling about your experiences with health challenges and how you can trust God in those situations. Reflect on the key verse and how it applies to your situation.

SHADOW OF DEATH

Have you ever overcome one significant challenge only to be hit with an even more severe and terrifying crisis? In this chapter, Sheldon and Annette face another health crisis that tests their faith and resilience to the limit.

Isaiah 41:10 (NLT):
"Don't be afraid, for I am with you. Don't be discouraged, for I am your God. I will strengthen you and help you. I will hold you up with my victorious right hand."

In this chapter, Sheldon and Annette struggle with an intense health crisis without clear medical answers. Despite the despair, they find strength and hope through faith, prayer, and the support of their spiritual community.

If you haven't read Chapter Nine, go do so now.

QUESTIONS FOR REFLECTION:

1. How did Sheldon's health crisis initially manifest, and what were the reactions of the doctors he visited?

2. What emotional impact did the loss of Lady's puppies have on Sheldon, and how did it contribute to his health decline?

3. How did the visit from pastors David and Nicole Crank influence Sheldon and Annette's next steps in seeking medical treatment?

4. What role did faith and prayer play in providing hope and support for Sheldon and Annette during this crisis?

5. How did Annette's role as a caregiver affect her spiritually and emotionally during Sheldon's health crisis?

PERSONAL REFLECTION QUESTIONS:

1. Reflect on a time when you felt overwhelmed by a health crisis or another form of intense stress. How did you find strength and support?

2. How do you handle situations where you don't have clear answers or solutions? What role does faith play in these moments?

3. In what ways can you support someone who is struggling with a severe health issue or another crisis?

4. How do you align your thoughts and words with God's truth during times of struggle? What practical steps can you take to maintain a positive and faith-filled mindset?

5. How does the key verse, Isaiah 41:10, speak to your current challenges?

ASK GOD TO SPEAK TO YOU:

Take a moment to pray and reflect on any health challenges or emotional pain you might be experiencing. Ask God to reveal any areas where you need His healing touch and guidance. Write down any thoughts or impressions you receive during this time of reflection.

NEXT STEPS:

1 **PRAYER:** Pray for God's healing and guidance in areas where you need physical and emotional restoration. Ask Him to help you trust His presence and protection.

2 **SHARE:** Talk with a trusted friend or mentor about your reflections and insights from this chapter. Discuss how you can support each other in seeking God's healing and strength during health crises.

3 **ACT:** Reach out to someone you know who is going through a difficult time. Share with them the key verse and your reflections, offering them hope and encouragement.

....

....

....

....

....

4 **REFLECT:** Write down your next steps and commit to following through. How can you apply what you've learned from this chapter to your current situation?

....

....

....

....

....

5 **JOURNAL:** Spend 10-15 minutes journaling about your experiences with health challenges and how you can trust God in those situations. Reflect on the key verse and how it applies to your situation.

AUTHOR AND FINISHER

Have you ever experienced a remarkable recovery in some area of your life? After facing severe health challenges, Sheldon witnesses a resurgence of prosperity and growth.

Philippians 1:6 (NLT):
"And I am certain that God, who began the good work within you, will continue his work until it is finally finished on the day when Christ Jesus returns."

In this chapter, Sheldon's recovery marked a new season of prosperity and growth, both personally and in business. Through faith and perseverance, he navigated the challenges and recognized Jesus as the author and finisher of his story, bringing transformation and triumph out of trials.

If you haven't read Chapter Ten, go do so now.

QUESTIONS FOR REFLECTION:

1. How did Sheldon's health recovery parallel the revival of their business?

2. What was Sheldon's initial reaction to Joseph's offer to buy the company, and how did his perspective change over time?

3. How did Sheldon's past choices and life experiences contribute to his current success and understanding of God's plan?

4. In what ways did Sheldon see God's hand in the people and events that shaped his journey?

5. How can recognizing Jesus as the author and finisher of our faith influence our outlook on life's challenges?

PERSONAL REFLECTION QUESTIONS:

1. Reflect on a time when you experienced a significant turnaround in your life. How did your faith play a role in that transformation?

2. How do you perceive God's role in the people and events that have shaped your journey?

3. What are some gifts and abilities that God has given you? How can you use them to fulfill His purpose in your life?

4. How can you shift your focus from your past mistakes to the future that God has planned for you?

5. How does the key verse, Philippians 1:6, speak to your current life situation?

ASK GOD TO SPEAK TO YOU:

Take a moment to pray and ask God to reveal His plans for your life. Reflect on the ways He has been the author and finisher of your faith journey. Write down any insights or messages you receive during this time of prayer.

NEXT STEPS:

1   **PRAYER:** Pray for God's guidance and strength to trust His plan for your life. Ask Him to help you see His hand in your past, present, and future.

2   **SHARE:** Share your reflections and insights with a trusted friend or mentor. Discuss how you can support each other in recognizing Jesus as the author and finisher of your faith.

3   **ACT:** Identify one area of your life where you can use your gifts and abilities to fulfill God's purpose. Take a step of faith to act on it this week.

4   **REFLECT:** Write down your next steps and commit to following through. How can you apply what you've learned from this chapter to your current situation?

5   **JOURNAL:** Spend 10-15 minutes journaling about your journey of faith and how you can keep your eyes on Jesus as the author and finisher of your faith. Reflect on the key verse and its significance in your life.

GOD OF MIRACLES

Have you ever wondered how many miracles God has performed in your life? In this chapter, Sheldon reflects on the numerous miracles God has performed in his life.

Jeremiah 32:27 (NLT): "I am the LORD, the God of all the peoples of the world. Is anything too hard for me?"

In this chapter, Sheldon recounts the miraculous interventions of God in his life, particularly highlighting a significant business crisis in 2015. Despite a major licensing oversight that threatened their business, God's guidance, favor, and timely provision through various people turned the situation around. Sheldon underscores the power of faith, perseverance, and the importance of recognizing and cooperating with God's miraculous work in our lives.

If you haven't read Chapter Eleven, go do so now.

QUESTIONS FOR REFLECTION:

1. How did Sheldon's company end up in a critical situation in Miami?

2. What role did Rosa play in the process of securing the license for S&S Waste?

3. How did Sheldon and his team respond to the challenges they faced from other waste-hauling companies?

4. In what ways did Sheldon see God's hand at work during this challenging period?

5. How can recognizing God's miracles in our own lives influence our faith and trust in Him?

PERSONAL REFLECTION QUESTIONS:

1. Reflect on a time when you experienced a miracle in your life. How did it impact your faith?

2. How do you see God's hand at work in the challenges you face today?

3. What are some ways you can strengthen your trust in God's plans for your life?

4. How can you share your experiences of God's miracles with others to encourage their faith?

5. What does the key verse, Jeremiah 32:27, mean to you personally in your current life situation?

ASK GOD TO SPEAK TO YOU:

Take a moment to pray and ask God to reveal His miracles in your life. Reflect on how He has been present in your journey and write down any insights or messages you receive during this time of prayer.

....

....

....

....

....

....

....

....

....

....

....

....

....

....

....

....

NEXT STEPS:

1 **PRAYER:** Pray for God's guidance and strength to trust His plans for your life. Ask Him to help you see His hand in your past, present, and future.

2 **SHARE:** Share your reflections and insights with a trusted friend or mentor. Discuss how you can support each other in recognizing and celebrating God's miracles.

3 **ACT:** Identify one area of your life where you need to trust God for a miracle. Take a step of faith to act on it this week.

4 **REFLECT:** Write down your next steps and commit to following through. How can you apply what you've learned from this chapter to your current situation?

5 **JOURNAL:** Spend 10-15 minutes journaling about the miracles you have experienced in your life. Reflect on the key verse and its significance in your journey of faith.

JUDGED WORTHY OF LOVE

Have you ever felt the weight of your identity tied to your achievements or failures? In this lesson, we'll explore how navigating the highs and lows of life can reveal deeper truths about our worth and identity. As we journey through Sheldon's story, we'll see how God's unconditional love and affirmation transform our understanding of self-worth.

Ephesians 2:10 (NLT): *"For we are God's masterpiece. He has created us anew in Christ Jesus, so we can do the good things he planned for us long ago."*

In this chapter, Sheldon reflects on the highs and lows of life, sharing how he learned to trust in God's plan through the sale of his business and the challenges that followed. He realizes that his worth isn't tied to his achievements but is found in God's unconditional love and affirmation.

If you haven't read Chapter Twelve, go do so now.

QUESTIONS FOR REFLECTION:

1. How did Sheldon's experiences of selling his business reveal underlying issues about his identity?

2. What challenges did Sheldon face in balancing his sense of self-worth after selling the business?

3. How did God use Sheldon's business journey to show His unconditional love and faithfulness?

4. What lessons did Sheldon learn about separating his identity from his work and achievements?

5. How can Sheldon's story encourage you to find your worth in God's love rather than in your accomplishments?

PERSONAL REFLECTION QUESTIONS:

1. Reflect on a time when you faced a major life change. How did it affect your sense of identity and worth?

2. In what ways have you tied your self-worth to your achievements or work? How has this impacted your life?

3. Consider a situation where you felt God's unconditional love and affirmation. How did it change your perspective?

4. How can you begin to see yourself as God's masterpiece, created for good works?

5. What steps can you take to find your worth and identity in Christ rather than in external achievements?

ASK GOD TO SPEAK TO YOU:

Take a moment to pray and reflect on the areas of your life where you seek worth and identity outside of God. Ask God to reveal any lies you believe about yourself and to help you find your true identity in Him. Write down any thoughts or impressions you receive during this time of reflection.

NEXT STEPS:

1 PRAYER: Pray for God's guidance in helping you find your worth and identity in His love. Ask Him to heal any areas where you feel unworthy or defined by your achievements.

2 SHARE: Talk with a trusted friend or mentor about your reflections and insights from this chapter. Discuss how you can support each other in finding your identity in Christ.

3 ACT: Identify one practical way you can remind yourself of your worth in God's eyes this week. It could be through affirmations, scripture reading, or acts of kindness.

4 REFLECT: What did God tell you to do? Write down your next steps and commit to following through.

5 JOURNAL: Spend 10-15 minutes journaling about your experiences with identity and self-worth. Reflect on the key verse and how it applies to your situation.

NEXT STEPS: MOVING FORWARD IN FAITH

Congratulations on completing the study guide for "Beneath the Rubble." This journey has been an opportunity to reflect, grow, and deepen your faith. As you move forward, here are some suggested next steps to continue your spiritual growth and share what you've learned with others:

1. TELL YOUR FRIENDS: Share the impact this book and study guide have had on your life. Encourage your friends and family to read "Beneath the Rubble" and use the study guide. Invest in their spiritual growth by buying them a copy and discussing your insights together.

2. START A SMALL GROUP: Consider starting a 12-week small group or Bible study to go through "Beneath the Rubble" together. Invite friends, family, or members of your church community to join you. Use this study guide as a framework for your discussions and reflections. Meeting regularly will provide ongoing support and accountability.

3. EMBRACE SALVATION: If you haven't already, consider making Jesus the Lord of your life. The Bible says in Romans 10:9 (NLT), "If you openly declare that Jesus is Lord and believe in your heart that God raised him from the dead, you will be saved." Pray this simple prayer: "Lord Jesus, I confess that I am a sinner in need of Your grace. I believe that You died for my sins and rose again. I invite You into my heart to be my Lord and Savior. Thank You for saving me. Amen." Share this decision with someone you trust and seek guidance on your new journey of faith.

4. KEEP SAYING "YES" TO GOD: Remain open to God's leading and continue to say "yes" to His plans for your life. Trust that He who began a good work in you will carry it on to completion (Philippians 1:6).

By taking these next steps, you'll be well-equipped to continue growing in your faith and sharing the love of Jesus with others. Remember, your journey with God is ongoing, and He has great plans for your future. Stay committed, stay connected, and keep moving forward in faith.

To order more copies visit
www.IgniteWealthSystems.com

www.IgniteWealthSystems.com

Made in the USA
Columbia, SC
21 October 2025